EVIL TWINS

A chilling book detailing the heinous crimes of some of the world's most evil twins

About the Author

Born in the outskirts of Dublin, Jon Lawson loved visiting the mobile library that visited his area every week as a youngster. Now a qualified criminologist, his obsession with true crime started at a very young age in those libraries. He now resides in the Florida with his wife and three teenage daughters. He dedicates this book to them.

To receive updates on new releases, freebies, flash sales and to get a free sneak preview of upcoming book Russian Serial Killers from Jon Lawson visit www.queenbeespublishing.com, enter your best email address and let us know you are interested in receiving true crime book updates.

Contents

Introduction

Twins tend to fascinate us for many different reasons, from their genetic makeup to the empathy they feel for one another. In many cases, one twin claims to be able to feel the pain when the other is hurt. This demonstrates the closeness of twins when it comes not only to appearance but emotions.

However, some twins do not stop at just emotional and facial similarities – they also form a bond of evil, carrying out heinous crimes against others and in some cases even against one another. The world has seen many cases of crimes committed by evil twins, perhaps one of the most famous set of evil twins being Ronnie and Reggie Kray. These London gangsters ruled the East End and went down in the annals of criminal history.

There are many other cases of serious crimes committed by twins, which have taken place in various countries all around the world. Take Robert and Jonathon Maskell, who at the age of just 18 robbed and killed their step-grandmother. Then there was George and Stefan Spitzer, who were found guilty of numerous counts of kidnap and rape.

Of course, it's not just male twins who are capable of committing such unthinkable crimes – there are also many cases of female twins who have carried out unspeakable acts. For instance, Betty Wilson and Peggy Lowe were twins who ended up being arrested for arranging the vicious beating and subsequent murder of a wealthy doctor – who just happened to be Betty's husband.

In this book, we look at these cases along with a number of other crimes that have been committed by twins. The acts that some of these twins committed shocked the world at the time, and even today these evil twins continue to fascinate us. From murder and matricide to contract killings and rape, evil twins have committed a variety of crimes that the world will never forget.

ROBERT AND JONATHAN MASKELL

These evil twins may have only killed one person, but this just happened to be a member of their own family – and they carried out the murder on their own 18th birthday

The Maskell twins

When identical twins, Robert and Jonathan Maskell, were born on 28th January 1987 nobody could have imagined that exactly eighteen years later the pair would be committing murder – and within the family. However, this is exactly what happened, with the pair leaving their own 18th birthday celebrations in order to carry out their heinous crime.

The two boys were from Edmonton in North London, England, and their childhood appears to have been quite unremarkable. However, as they grew older they did not have much success in life, as they suffered from learning difficulties, found it difficult to make friends, were described as outcasts and geeks, and as they moved into their late teens they also found it extremely difficult to get and keep a job.

One thing that the twins did enjoy doing, however, was spending time on Internet chat rooms and MSN. Here, they not only developed but shared various fantasies, living in their own little online bubble and allegedly trying to impress underage girls who were also using the chat facilities online. Life in the real world, however, was very different and the twins found themselves struggling on a number of levels, including intellectually, emotionally and financially.

The adopted grandmother

While Robert and Jonathan did not have many friends, one constant figure in their lives was Anjelica Hallwood, who was their adoptive grandmother. Although she wasn't blood related, Anjelica had taken the twins on as her own grandchildren and had always treated them as her own. Many said that she only ever showed the boys kindness and love, which makes their crime even more difficult to understand. Anjelica was originally from Malta and was not even five feet tall. It was this frail, tiny and loving lady that

ended up paying the price for the twins' greed
and evil ways despite all of the kindness she had
shown to them.

Mrs Hallwood's downfall was that she kept a
considerable amount of money in her home and
the twins knew all about this. They came up with
what they believed was a cunning plan to rob the
old lady – something that they had done
previously the year before the murder. However,
the bungled robbery resulted in not only the
death of a sweet old woman but the
imprisonment of the two boys who had literally
just turned eighteen at the time of the crime.

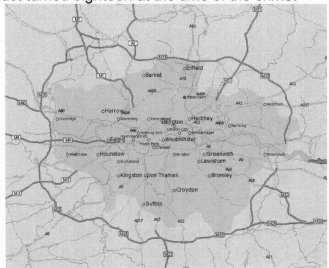

Edmonton, London

The murder of Anjelica Hallwood

By the time they reached their 18th birthdays, the
Maskell twins were in a position where they had
no prospects, no jobs, and no money. They had

very few friends but one of the ones they did have was about to find himself involved in both robbery and murder at a time when he should have been enjoying celebrating the twins' 18th birthday with them.

In 2004, the twins are said to have stolen around £800 from their step-grandmother and they were therefore aware that she kept money in her small flat in Edmonton. Having lost their last job at the Paradise Park Zoo after they crashed a jeep, the twins found themselves unable to get work and were becoming pretty desperate for cash by the time their 18th birthday rolled around in January 2005. The £800 stolen the year before was long spent and penniless the two boys had to come up with an idea to replenish their finances.

What they decided to do was turn to their friend, nineteen year old Dwane Johnston, who was their half-sister's boyfriend and had only been released from prison that same morning after doing a stint for driving offences. The three boys spent the day plotting and conniving in order to come up with a plan to break into the old lady's flat and steal the money she kept there. This was made all the easier by the fact that Johnston was actually staying at the flat with Anjelica following his prison release.

A party was being held for the twins at their family home on 28th January 2005 but they sneaked out and met up with Johnston. The three of them then made their way to Hallwood's flat under the cover of darkness. According to reports, just minutes after they had entered the flat, neighbours heard banging and loud noises coming from the property. This comes as no surprise since, at the time, the three boys were raiding the flat and putting an end to the Anjelica's life.

It is reported that while the twins concentrated their efforts on pulling bags of money out of the old woman's wardrobe, Johnston took the opportunity to punch her repeatedly in the face. He is also said to have suffocated her while she lay on the floor by forcing his forearm into her neck. It was later revealed in court that the pensioner had been punched so hard that many of her facial bones had been shattered.

As a final insult, the three boys scattered treasured photographs belonging to Hallwood all over the hallway before making their getaway. Astoundingly, even though they had just left the pensioner – the woman they used to call Nana – for dead, they had the gall to stop off and try to purchase mobile phone credit using the stolen money. However, the shop owner told them that some of it was no longer legal tender so they had to leave without their credit.

A spending spree

The three boys had been expecting to find a tidy stash of money at the flat, as it was thought that Anjelica kept several thousand pounds in bags in her wardrobe. However, the amount that they boys actually found was £1000, which is

apparently all that the pensioner's life was worth
to the boys. While the money may not have been
as much as they'd hoped, this didn't stop them
from attempting a shopping spree. In fact, after
leaving the old lady for dead they bought kebabs
and then returned to the party as though nothing
had happened. Sometime later, they were also
caught on CCTV as they enjoyed a shopping trip
using the stolen money. The footage showed the
boys laughing and joking as they spent the
money that they had taken from the dead
woman.

It was also revealed that while on the shopping
trip Jonathan spent £170 of the stolen cash to
buy a mobile phone. However, he was reportedly
mugged by a hoodie on the way home and the
phone was stolen from him. Without a second
thought, he simply took more of the money from
his home where he'd stashed it and then went
out and replaced the phone.

Finding the body

The morning after the murder, the daughter of
the victim, Joan Hallwood, went to visit her mom
at the flat. She was concerned when she kept
knocking at the door but received no response.
Bizarrely, Johnston was around to act as a Good
Samaritan and slip the security chain for Ms.
Hallwood. She was then faced with a devastating
sight – that of her mother's dead body and a flat
that had been totally ransacked.

According to reports, the dead woman had blankets and clothing thrown all over her. There were also drawers that had been emptied out on the floor, the wardrobe had been smashed open and the flat was a complete mess. Ms. Hallwood was naturally in shock but unbeknown to her at the time, the killers of her mother would soon be caught because they made what can only be described as clumsy yet common mistakes.

Caught!

There were a number of factors that contributed to the twins and Johnston being charged and sent down, although they did only get charged with robbery and manslaughter rather than murder. Firstly, the boys had left fingerprints and even a boot print inside the property when they carried out the raid.

More damning evidence against the twins and Johnston came because, like many other criminals, they couldn't resist bragging about their crime to try and impress others. In this case, it was two girls that they were trying to impress, one of whom was Robert's girlfriend, Siobhan Henderson, and the other a teen who used to engage in phone sex with Jonathan, Hayley Rance.

According to Henderson, who later told her story to authorities, Robert had told her that he and his brother had killed their grandmother. He claimed to have beaten her and then attacked her with a hammer according to his girlfriend. She said that at first she didn't believe him but he was insistent and his brother also started claiming the same thing.

The boys were further incriminated by Dwane Johnston, who at first was being treated as a witness in the case. However, his story started to fall apart and before long he was spilling the beans to officers and claiming that it was the twins that set up the whole robbery. He stated that Jonathan had told him that they were planning to rob their Nana because she kept cash in the wardrobe.

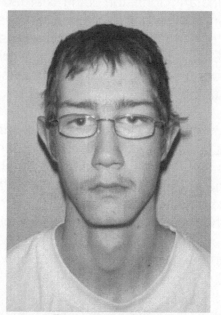

Dwane Johnston

Trial and sentencing

When it came to the trial at the Old Bailey, the twins didn't give evidence. They went from denying having any part in the killing through to blaming one another for Nana's death. Following the trial, all three of the boys were cleared of the old lady's murder. However, they were charged with robbery and manslaughter, each of them receiving nine years behind bars for their part in the crime.

Judge Gerald Gordon, who presided at the trial, stated that he couldn't imagine a crime that was more despicable. He added that the boys could easily have carried out the robbery when Mrs. Hallwood was out and safe but instead they chose to carry out the crime while she was in the flat in the full knowledge that they would have to restrain her.

Following the sentencing, the pensioner's son, Peter Hallwood, spoke outside the court. He said: "I am struggling to cope with the knowledge that the twins and Johnston were capable of doing this. They are the lowest of the low, cold and callous, and I can't believe they would bite the hand that feeds them."

ROBERT AND STEPHEN SPAHALSKI

Identical twins, Robert and Stephen Spahalski, were both killers. However, unlike many other evil twins, they did not kill as a pair but independently from one another

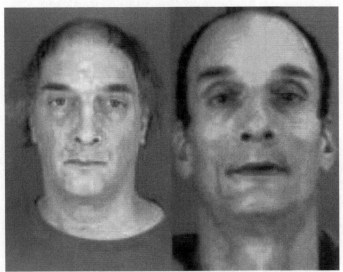

The Spahalski twins

Like many other sets of twins, Robert and Stephen Spahalski had a reputation for doing a lot of things together including engaging in dubious activities such as petty crime and drug taking. However, the one thing that they did independently from one another was to take human lives. In fact, when he found out what his twin had been up to over the years, Stephen – who was the first of the brothers to kill and be imprisoned – told authorities 'I thought I was the only murderer in the family'.

Born in 1955 in Elmira, New York, the Spahalski twins were torn apart in their mid-teens after Stephen killed the owner of a store. While he had become a killer at the tender age of just sixteen what he didn't realize was that nearly two decades on his twin brother would go a step further and become a serial killer. During their early and mid-teens the twins acted together in committing various crimes in order to fund their drug habits. However, these crimes were just a taste of things to come, as both brothers ended up behind bars for taking innocent lives.

Stephen Spahalski: Murder and incarceration

The first of the two twins to kill was Stephen – a man who was destined to spend the next few decades mostly incarcerated not just for the killing but also for robbery, kidnapping and violating his parole.

In 1971, Stephen was arrested for stabbing a 48 year old Elmira Heights store owner, Ronald Ripley, to death. He apparently told authorities that the man 'deserved it' and went on to claim that Ripley had made sexual advances towards him. At first, Robert had been suspected of carrying out the killing. However, Stephen pleaded guilty to manslaughter and served 8 years behind bars at Attica Prison in the state of New York. There were suspicions that while

Robert may not have carried out the crime he was present at the time.

After being released following the manslaughter charge, Stephen went back to his life of crime. Although he didn't kill again, he was back behind bars within a year of release for robbery and kidnapping. This time he served a longer sentence, and was not released until 1999. However, within a matter of months he was back in prison yet again, this time for violating his parole.

During all these years, Stephen was unaware that his brother had been forging a career for himself as a serial killer. It was only in 2005 that he was informed that his brother had been arrested on suspicion of multiple killings. In 2006 he applied for parole but this was denied because he would not take part in a programme for violent offenders, which prison officials wanted him to participate in. He was finally released in 2009 but just six months later was back behind bars after he walked in to the Five Star bank in Elmira and attempted to rob it just weeks after it had been robbed by another criminal.

New York

Elmira, New York

Robert Spahalski: Serial Killer

Robert Spahalski's murderous tendencies may not have come to light as early as his twin brother's but he certainly made up for that by making sure he really made his mark in the annals of criminal history.

While he did not begin his murder rampage until 1990, nearly two decades after his twin brother killed Ripley, Robert had been involved in a variety of criminal activities for years. He and his twin used to commit criminal acts together in their early and mid-teens in order to pay for the drugs that they had become addicted to. He also had a criminal record for arson dating back to 1971 after he set fire to the school. He was known to have a serious drug addiction and some said that he was also HIV positive.

In 1990, the naked body of a 24 year old woman, Moraine Armstrong, was discovered by police at her Lake Avenue apartment in Elmira. The date was 31st December 1990 and the woman was found with electrical cord wrapped around her neck. Despite their best efforts, police were unable to identify her killer and the case went cold – until many years later when Robert Spahalski – who had lived across the street from Armstrong at the time of the murder – confessed to authorities having already been detained on other murder charges.

In the summer of 1991, the body of a drug using prostitute, Adrian Berger, was discovered at her home in Emerson Street. The body appeared to have been there for some time and the thermostat at the flat was turned up full despite the fact that it was summer. As a result of these factors, the body was badly decomposed by the time it was found and police were unable to determine a cause of death. The death was not labelled as homicide – until, of course, Robert Spahalski confessed to the murder years later.

In October 1991, Robert took his murderous criminal activities to a whole new level after murdering a man and then taking his identity. He visited the home of 40 year old Charles Grande but ended up attacking him with a hammer and hitting him over the head. He stated later that this was because Grande refused to pay him $20 for sex. In order to try and throw police off the track, Spahalski turned the temperature in the property up full in a bid to aid the decomposition of the body. However, Rochester police pulled Robert up on a traffic stop before Grande's death had even come to light. Since he was driving Grande's car at the time, Robert showed the police the dead man's driving license and pretended that he was in fact Charles Grande.

When Charles' body finally was discovered, Robert was placed under arrest for trying to impersonate him during the traffic stop. However, the charges never stuck and in the summer of 1992 Robert was acquitted.

Robert's final kill and confession

The final known killing carried out by Robert Spahalski occurred years later on 4th November 2005. Robert was with his 54 year old next door neighbour and friend, Vivian Irizarry and the two of them were smoking crack cocaine. At the time, Robert's girlfriend of ten years, Christine Gonzalez, had gone to work so he and Vivian were alone in the property. According to his statement to police, Vivian took a knife in order to open a bag of crack cocaine and suddenly Spahalski 'freaked out' because what he saw was not his friend and neighbour but a demon. At this point he started beating her over the head with a hammer but once he started to come down from the drug induced frenzy, he found her convulsing on the floor. Robert claims that he then tried to put her out of her misery by strangling her to death.

Following the murder of Irizarry, Spahalski spent the rest of the weekend taking drugs. He then made his way to the police department in Rochester and turned himself in, advising authorities where the body of his friend and neighbour could be found. Had he not turned himself in, there is no telling whether he would have been caught or whether he would have continued to murder.

Victim – Vivian Irizarry

Unsolved murders

While Robert was convicted of murder in these four cases, there have been many other unsolved homicides in the same sort of area during the time when Spahalski was 'active'. This includes many women who were found strangled, stabbed or both in various locations in the area. There are said to be more than 30 unsolved homicides in the area where Robert's three female victims had lived with many taking place between 1990 and 2003 and bearing striking similarities to the Spahalski murders.

The mother of one of the victims actually identified Robert Spahalski as the man she saw her daughter with before she went missing. The 21 year old was later found dead behind a building having been both strangled and stabbed. Another woman, Hortence Greatheart, was found strangled at her apartment – the same apartment block where Spahalski lived on and off for nearly 15 years until he and his girlfriend were evicted in 2005. When Greatheart's body was found, the heating thermostat in her apartment had been turned up full.

Between 1991 and 2005 there were no known murders committed by Robert Spahalski. However, it is not in the nature of most serial killers to take such a lengthy break – and how many of the unsolved murders that took place

between these periods were down to him
remains a mystery.

PETE AND PAT BONDURANT

Twin brothers from the small town of Elkton, Tennessee, Pete and Pat Bondurant were not only known as drug lords but they went on to commit a series of grisly murders

The Bondurant Twins

Born on April 4th 1955, Hugh and Kenneth Bondurant were twin brothers who are said to have been bullied at school as kids because they became morbidly obese at a young age. The brothers went by their middle names, calling themselves Pete and Pat (for Patterson). Little did anyone guess that these two overweight, bullied twins would go on to not only become known as drug lords in their town of Elkton, Tennessee but would also acquire a cult following of youngsters and would eventually commit a series of violent murders.

Like many other evil twins, the first killings carried out by these two brothers were not performed as a pair. It was actually Pete who was the first to kill – one of his own friends in

1975. He had moved to Cincinnati after graduating from High School at the age of 18, leaving his twin brother behind in Elkton. However, Pete did not fare well without his twin around and started drinking a lot. He went on two stab not one but two of his friends, and one of them died as a result of no fewer than forty stab wounds. Pete was then convicted of manslaughter and put behind bars.

In the meantime, his twin brother Pat was actually doing pretty well in his hometown. He had secured a decent job and met a woman – their bizarre meeting occurred after she crashed into the back of his car. Three years later they were married and went on to have two children. Everything seemed to be going pretty well for Pat – that was until Pete Bondurant was released from jail on parole and decided to return to his twin brother back in Elkton.

Downward spiral

While Pete Bondurant had already started his murderous career – although his conviction was actually for manslaughter – Pat's life may have turned out very differently had his twin not returned to his hometown. Unfortunately, he did return and this was the start of a slippery slope for both brothers. Pete moved into the farmhouse where Pat and his wife, Denise, lived and this soon became a den of iniquity. Youngsters who seemed to admire and follow the twins were coming and going from the property at all hours and according to reports there were all sorts of drugs freely available as well as alcohol.

Bondurant farmhouse (no longer in this location)

A busy year for the twins

It seems that being drug lords, corrupting the young, drinking and partying simply wasn't enough to keep the twins satisfied. This was proven in 1986, when it appears that the two men had a very busy year – a year of killing. There were three known killings that took place over the course of the year, one far more detailed than the others due to the presence of a key witness – Pat's wife, Denise. The murder of Gwen Dugger was the first one that the twins were indicted for in 1990, although it was not long before details of the other murders were revealed.

Gwen Dugger was the young 23 year old mother of a young boy. She was devoted to her son, so much so that she actually kept his baby diaper pin attached to the lace of her tennis shoe to symbolise her love for the boy. One evening in May 1986, she went to the rundown farmhouse where the twins and Denise were living along with her younger brother who had to collect his car from the property.

Pete seemed to take a liking to Gwen and within a short period of time had persuaded her to stay on at the property for a while. Her brother, not suspecting anything was wrong, had no qualms about taking his car and driving off, leaving his sister at the property – and at the mercy of the twins. Over the course of the evening, Pete gave Gwen various drugs until she was incapacitated. He then took her into the bathroom intending to have sex with her, and his twin brother decided to join them. However, Denise walked in to find her husband Pat having sex with the woman, who was almost unconscious by this time, and understandably she was unhappy.

According to reports, Denise later tried to persuade Gwen, who was still passed out on the floor, to leave and go home. However, at that moment Pat came over and using the handle of an axe started to beat Gwen mercilessly. Pete then decided to do his bit and taking a 22-calibre shotgun he fired two bullets into the young mother to 'put her out of her misery'.

The indignity that was showered upon this young mother did not stop with her death. The twins then took her body to the Elk River and stuffed it into a 55 gallon drum. They then set fire to it, letting it burn until it was nothing more than bone fragments and ash. The remains were then dumped into the river. They also went on to burn a mattress that had been on the floor of the farmhouse but left a pile of debris from the burning. This would be part of their undoing, for it was here that forensic officers later found damning evidence – the diaper pin that Gwen used to wear on her shoe.

Victim – Gwen Dugger

Other murders committed the same year

Although these murders did not come to light until later on, the twins are said to have committed another two murders during 1986. The first was down to Pat, who had apparently beaten to death a co-worker named Ronnie Gaines. He admitted this to his wife, Denise, who later told authorities after she and Pat had split up. His also confessed that after he had killed the man, Pete had helped him to dispose of the body by burning it and the remains had been buried in his parents' cabin yard at West Point.

The same year saw Pete Bondurant kill a former girlfriend named Terry Lynn Clarke. While the details of this death appear to be limited, he was later charged with the murder while already serving time for the murder of Gwen Dugger.

The confession of Denise Bondurant

After the murder of Gwen Dugger, Denise had to help the twins to clean up the blood from the farmhouse and scrub the floors. She later told authorities that she had to do this because she was terrified of them and what they might do to her. Meanwhile, the family of the unfortunate young mother still had no idea what had happened to her and were putting up posters in the area in a bid to try and find out more information.

Over the next few years, Denise split up from Pat Bondurant and in 1990 she finally found the courage to go to the authorities and tell them about the murder of Gwen Dugger. Granted immunity by the police, she explained what had happened that evening and why she had helped the twins to clean up the farmhouse after disposing of the body. She provided a detailed explanation of how the young mum had been killed and what the twins had done to dispose of the body and try to get rid of any evidence.

In addition to this, Denise also now knew about the killing of Ronnie Gaines. Pat had told her all about killing his co-worker and had also implicated his twin by telling Denise that Pete had helped him to burn the body and bury the remains.

While the twins had by now moved from the farmhouse where the Gwen Dugger murder had taken place, Denise took police officers and forensics to the scene of the crime. Using a chemical that is able to show up blood traces that are invisible to the naked eye, luminal, investigators were able to see that there had definitely been a grisly crime committed. One author who studied the case, John White, stated that 'the room lit up like the night sky' when the chemical was used.

The indictment and imprisonment

In 1990, evil twins, Pete and Pat Bondurant, were finally indicted and their trial began in 1991. Despite the shocking brutality with which they ended the life of a young mother, they were only charged with second degree murder rather than first degree murder for the death of Gwen Dugger. This was because there was no body due to the twins having burned it and thrown whatever was left into the river.

The twins were sentenced to 25 years each for the second degree murder charge. However, while serving this sentence, Pete Bondurant was also convicted in the murder of his former girlfriend, Terry Lynn Clarke. Also while serving his sentence, Pat Bondurant was charged with first degree murder for the killing of Ronnie Gaines.

Although the twins had originally been sentenced to 25 years each for Gwen Dugger's murder, this changed when they were charged with the additional deaths. Pat is not scheduled to be released until 2070, which means one less evil twin on the streets of America for many decades to come. The news is not so good when it comes to his twin brother Pete, who is described as the most dominant and violent tempered of the two. He is scheduled for release in 2018.

GEORGE AND STEFAN SPITZE

In the late 1990s, twin brothers George and Stefan Spitzer were handed down maximum sentences for felonies including the kidnapping, drugging and date rape of women. Their response? That they may have been 'jerks' to women but they weren't criminals

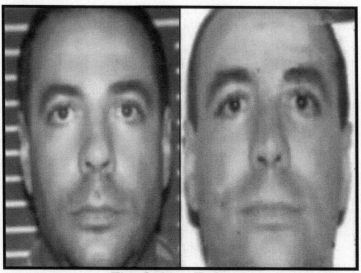

The Spitzer Twins

Being smooth-talkers, having relatively good looks, and boasting the ability to attract the attention of women are three of the key qualities that twin brothers George and Stefan Spitzer had. However, it was these three qualities – plus their unscrupulous natures and lack of remorse – that led them to a life of crime. Kidnapping, drugging women, and date rape are amongst the felonies that the twin brothers were found guilty of when they were sentenced – and they received the maximum sentences from the judge. Their crimes have also led to them becoming known as the 'Roofie Romeos' due to their habit of using the date rape drug Rohypnol to enable them to assault women.

Brought up in Communist Romania, George and Stefan Spitzer had big ambitions before they turned to crime. The identical twin brothers wanted to head to Hollywood and become big stars, enjoying worldwide fame. They did manage to make their way to Hollywood and they did get the worldwide fame they craved so much. However, this was not because they became big stars – it was because they became sexual predators who used drugs, violence and even videotapes in order to assault and have sex with women.

Date Raping

It was clear that these twin brothers did not struggle when it came to getting a date. They had the charm, character and personalities to get dates with women with ease. Unfortunately, these desirable qualities and traits were merely a front for their sexual perversions when it came to women. According to reports, the two brothers knocked out close to thirty women with Rohypnol, which has become known as a date rape drug but was actually used to aid sleep and relieve back pain. Unfortunately, this drug also has the ability to turn women into obedient sex slaves, which is something that George and Stefan used to their advantage.

During the day, the two brothers worked as car salesmen, which meant that they always had access to flashy cars – another major attraction for young women. However, when they went out on dates with women they would make up whole new lives for themselves. Stefan used to tell his dates that he was a wealthy movie mogul, so it was not surprising that they had no qualms about taking drinks off him or even heading back to his place. George used to convince his dates that he was a psychologist, which again instilled trust in the women that he was with because they thought he was a doctor. The twins actually lived in a fantasy world and these were not the only lies they came up with. On other occasions Stefan had claimed to be the youngest commercial airline pilot ever employed while George claimed to be the rich owner of a Toyota dealership. The pair even bragged to women about being martial arts experts who had trained none other than the Muscles from Brussels, Jean-Claude Van Damme.

However, what the unfortunate women didn't know was that not only were these two brothers lying through their teeth but that they were using a powerful drug to spike their food and drinks in order to have their wicked way with them, whether they were willing partners or not. It was eventually revealed that not only were the twins drugging and sexually assaulting these women but that they were also videotaping all of the

attacks – something that gave the police the
evidence they were looking for when their crimes
finally came to light. All of their crimes took place
between 1993 and 1996 when they were in their
late 30s. They were actually sentenced at the
age of 41.

Sadly, although many women had been
assaulted by the Spitzer twins by the time their
string of sex crimes was unveiled, most did not
report what had happened to them until after the
twins had been arrested because they were too
embarrassed. These were usually very savvy
women who went on the dates in their own cars,
made sure they met their dates somewhere
public and did not overindulge when it came to
drinking. Despite all of this, the method used by
the Spitzer brothers turned them into easy prey.

Rumbled

 The brothers were finally rumbled after George
met up with a 36 year old air hostess named
Linda. She met up with the seemingly charming
man in Santa Monica at the World Cafe. Here,
the pair decided to eat some pasta and enjoyed
a bottle of red wine between them. Throughout
the meal, George – who referred to himself as
Gino – bragged relentlessly about how he was
both a marketing expert and a doctor of
psychology. He also bragged about his brother
being a rich and famous movie producer.

World Café, Santa Monica

All of this bragging actually made his date feel
quite uneasy and according to her later
statements she started to find the whole evening
quite boring. At around 10pm she decided that
she wanted to leave. However, she later told
authorities that everything after this was a total
blank. The next thing she remembers is waking
up next to George at nearly 6am with a banging
headache. She was completed naked and as she
looked over at her clothes she knew that she
hadn't removed them herself because of how
dishevelled they were. George tried to convince
her that they hadn't had sex and the only reason
he had brought her back was because she'd got
terrible hiccups and he wanted to give her
something to stop them.

Unsurprisingly, Linda was not convinced about
anything that George told her and later on during

the same day she went to the authorities. Her suspicions resulted in the police heading to the house that the twins were living in and here they made a shocking discovery. No fewer than seven cases of the drug Rohypnol were discovered at the property along with a computer that had dozens of women's names on the database. Most damning of all was the collection of video tapes that authorities found at the property – more than twenty homemade porno videos that showed the two brothers having sex with various women who had been drugged.

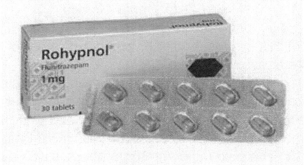

Rohypnol

Cops inundated with calls from victims

George Spitzer was quickly arrested following Linda's report to the police and the discovery of items that were found at the house. Within a matter of days, police in Los Angeles found themselves being inundated with calls from women who claimed that they had also fallen victim to date rape and assault from the two brothers over the past few years. In total, 26 women gave statements to the prosecution, as Linda's bravery in reporting her suspicions had made them realise that they needed to stop the monsters before any further women were attacked.

One woman told prosecutors that she was being fed potato chips by Stefan when she started feel as though she was in a dream. She went on to state that she vaguely remembers being taken to their house and assaulted but couldn't remember which of the twins had carried out the attack. This was a problem that many of the women had – trying to work out which of the brothers had assaulted them because they were identical and shared the same DNA. However, some claimed that they had been assaulted by both of the brothers simultaneously after being drugged.

Another victim who had been seeing George back in 1995 said that she later discovered that she had actually been sleeping with both of the brothers. She also told authorities that the twins had tried to justify this by telling her that they were from the same mother and shared the same blood.

Sentencing

Following these further statements from other victims, it wasn't long before Stefan was also arrested over the assaults and rapes. At the age of 41, the two brothers were found guilty of fifteen felony counts between them, eight being attributed to George and seven to Stefan. The

Judge at Santa Monica Superior Court, Richard
Neidorf, was quick to describe the brothers as
being a 'danger to society' and was also very
quick to hand down maximum sentences.
George received sixty years behind bars while
his twin brother was sentenced to just over thirty-
seven years.

At their hearing, the brothers tried to claim that
they were innocent, despite the presence of the
damning evidence that was found at their home.
They even told the judge that while they may
have been 'jerks' to women, they had not
committed any crime. Given the fact that they
clearly believed drugging, kidnapping, assault
and date rape constituted nothing more than
being 'jerks' it is just as well that the judge
decided to keep them behind bars for many
decades to come.

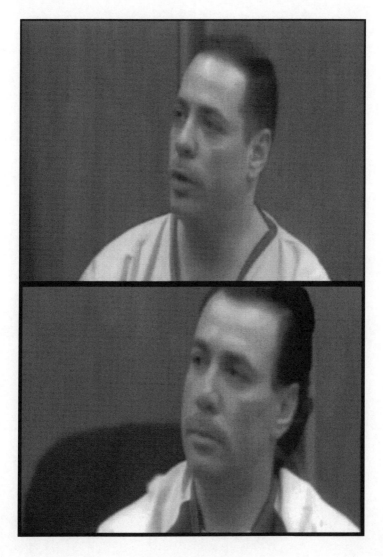

TYRONE AND JERONE SOTOLONGO

At the tender age of just nineteen, twin brothers Tyrone and Jerone Sotolongo found themselves under arrest for murder, attempted murder, and weapons charges – and under suspicion for three additional homicides and several other shootings

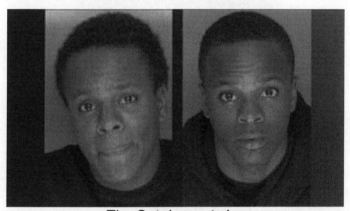

The Sotolongo twins

In 2013, two young men – twin brothers aged just nineteen – found themselves being taken in by police officers in Stockton. One of the twins, Tyrone Sotolongo, was arrested and charged with both murder and attempted murder while the other twin, Jerone, was taken in on weapons related charges. In addition to this, a 28 year old female accomplice, Taneisha Ivy, was also arrested with the twins on drug related charges.

Taneisha Ivy

However, this was just the tip of the iceberg, as authorities quickly revealed that they had reason to believe that one or both brothers were also involved in three other homicides as well as three shootings. However, with the teens being twins, the police had one big problem...they had no idea which of the two was involved in which of these crimes.

The arrest of Tyrone Sotolongo was in relation to a drive-by shooting in December 2012, which resulted in the death of a 21 year old man, Eric Madison. However, the week after they boys were arrested, Jerone tried to deny being involved in any killings, stating that the authorities were just trying whatever they could in order to try and take him and his brother down for something that they weren't even involved in. He was quick to admit that he had engaged in a variety of criminal acts, such as drug dealing, but said that he had never killed.

This was not the opinion of Stockton police officials, who had strong suspicions that the twins were involved in two unsolved 2012 homicides as well as one in 2011. This included the killing of a 60 year old man, Armando Pina, who was shot and killed in broad daylight in the Victory Park area in 2012 over his gold chain. In addition to these homicides, police were also linking the brothers to a number of non-fatal shootings in the area.

Residents in Victory Park mourning Armando Pina

Gang members and serial killers

Before being arrested by Stockton police over the drive-by shooting and weapons charges, the twins were already documented gang members. Following their arrest, John Phillips, a criminologist, described them as 'serial killers' due to the fact that they were being connected to a number of unsolved murders in the area.

While many kids of their age were still studying, living at home with parents, and deciding what they wanted to do by way of a career, the Sotolongo brothers' lives were already mapped out – and being banged up behind bars was to feature strongly in their future. In stark contrast to most other kids their age, the boys stood accused or murder, shootings, drugs related charges and more.

Although the Sotolongo brothers had been taken in by police over the drive-by shooting and weapons charges, police were unable to pin the other crimes on them at that time because there was no hard evidence to link them to the shootings and additional homicides. Officials stated at the time that it was not a simple process because although authorities believed that one or both brothers were involved in the other crimes it was a challenge to work out which one – a problem that authorities often have when it comes to crimes committed by identical twins.

At that stage the police informed the media that more investigations needed to be carried out before the twins could be charged with any additional crimes. They also appealed to the community to come forward with any information that they might have with regards to the twins' connection to any of these other crimes. In the meantime, the teenage boys were held in San

Joaquin County Jail and bail was set at $4.75 million for Tyrone and $1.35 million for Jerone. Officials hoped that by setting bail at this level and ensuring that the boys stood no chance of being bailed, members of the community would have more confidence about coming forward with any information.

Ongoing investigation

At the time of writing, authorities still appear to be investigating the link between the two brothers and the three additional homicides that occurred in 2011 and 2012 as well as the shootings that they were suspected of being involved in. Without the necessary evidence and witness testimony that police were hoping to be able to get, it will undoubtedly be very difficult to make any charges stick no matter how convinced the authorities are about the twins' involvement. Sadly, as is all too often the case, many people who do know information that could lead to something more solid are afraid to come forward because of the boys' involvement with gangs and their track records for violence and crime, which means that eventually the Sotolongo twins could effectively end up getting away with murder.

JAS AND TAS WHITEHEAD

For most teenage girls, their mothers are also their best friends. However, for unruly twin sisters, Jas and Tas Whitehead, their mother was to become their murder victim when they put an end to her life at the age of just sixteen

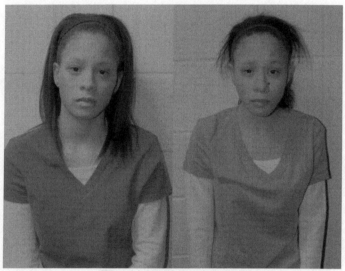

The Whitehead twins

In January 2010, an attractive young beautician from Conyers in Rockdale County, Georgia, was found dead in a pool of blood in the bath at her home. The young mother of twin girls was aged just thirty four years old when she was beaten and stabbed to death in her very own home. Worse still, it was later to emerge that the perpetrators of this heinous act were none other than her own twin daughters, sixteen year old Tasmiyah and Jasmiyah Whitehead.

When most people think of evil twins they tend to imagine adults and often male twins. However, as Jas and Tas demonstrated, there can be pure evil lurking behind the most innocent of faces. Having said that, after the murder of their mother, Jarmecca 'Nikki' Whitehead, some people actually came forward to state that they suspected the twins, so their attempts to play the young, innocent victims did not really go as planned.

In fact, although the two girls may have been young, they were far from innocent. As teenagers, they had become unruly, stubborn, argumentative, and extremely difficult, making life increasingly difficult for their mother. Jarmecca had raised the girls on her own, and by all accounts had done a good job at some point because both girls were once honours students as well as Girl Scouts. However, all of that changed as they moved into their early teens and decided that they had the right to live their lives as they wished to despite their young age.

Living with great-grandma

There are many kids that are sent to live with their grandparents or great-grandparents for one reason or another, and this is exactly what happened to Jas and Tas at around the age of fourteen. The reason that they were sent to live with their great-grandmother was more serious than in most other cases – it was because they physically assaulted their mother and the police ended up getting involved.

This incident led to the twins being sent to live with their great-grandmother, Della Frazier, who was eighty years of age, for close to two years. In fact, at the time of the killing they had only been back with their mother for a number of days after leaving their great-grandmother's at the age of sixteen.

During their time living with their great-grandmother, the two girls took full advantage of the old lady's frailty and age. They would run rings around her, knew that they could get away with anything, and pretty much ran her ragged. The girls are also said to have stolen $200 from her while staying with her. In fact, Frazier apparently even bought a deadbolt for her bedroom to stop Jas and Tas from getting in and rifling through her belongings in order to steal from her. It seems that their lack of respect for their elders – members of their own family – spanned generations.

Naturally, at the ripe old age of eighty, the twins' great-grandmother found it difficult to cope with the two girls. In addition to this, their mother – the doomed Jarmecca – was eager to try and build bridges with the twins and become a full time mother to them again. Friends of the beautician said that she made it clear that she wanted to start over with Jas and Tas and eventually arrangements were made for the girls to leave their great-grandmother's and return to live with their mother.

The return home

Sixteen year old Jas and Tas Whitehead finally returned home to their mother in January 2010, which must have been some sort of relief for their great-grandmother. The elderly woman had fallen victim to theft at the hands of the girls as well as being walked all over by them, but surely their mother would now be able to control them. Alas, this was never going to happen and, despite her eagerness to start afresh with her two girls, Jarmecca wouldn't even survive long enough to build the bridges that she so desperately wanted to.

Yucca Harris, one of Jarmecca's best friends, said that on the last night she'd seen her alive the beautician had told her that she was determined to fight for the girls. Harris said that she had been invited to a welcome home dinner at Jarmecca's home, which was being held in honour of the girls' return. This was just five days prior to the killing. Harris went on to tell officials that everyone had agreed to start afresh and that she'd spoken to Jas and Tas, telling them that they could call her whenever they needed to talk to somebody. She added that she thought she'd managed to get through to the twins but clearly that was not the case.

Finding the body – and the killers

Just days after their return home from their great-grandmother's, the twins came home from school to find their mother dead in the bath. They flagged down a passing police car for help and pretty soon officers were swarming over the house. Of course, an investigation was launched and it was not long before officials realized that the injuries that had been afflicted on the deceased pointed to two specific suspects – the victim's own daughters. Just four months after the death of Jarmecca, Jas and Tas Whitehead – still aged just sixteen – were arrested.

A number of factors had aroused suspicion amongst investigators in the case, such as CCTV footage that showed the girls getting into a car on the morning of the death at a time when they had told police they were at school. More damning was the evidence that came from bite marks on the twins' arms, which were examined by a dental expert. He was able to confirm that they matched the teeth of the deceased, their mother. On top of all this, there had been no forced entry at the property so police were pretty sure that whoever had killed the woman had known her and had easy access to the property.

The twins were arrested over the killing in May 2010 and initially both of them denied being involved in the incident. While they were detained awaiting trial, the two girls were separated so that they could not collude and come up with a story to try and convince a jury of their innocence. They continued to tell one lie after another in a bid to make authorities believe that they had not been involved. However, despite their heinous act these were essentially two young girls and they soon started tripping up on their own lies.

What actually happened to Jarmecca Whitehead?

In January 2014, a full four years following the killing, Tas Whitehead finally admitted to a number of criminal acts, one of which was the voluntary manslaughter of her mother. Originally, she was facing charges of murder along with her twin sister but her plea to lesser charges was accepted by the District Attorney's Office.

Now aged twenty, she was sentenced to thirty years behind bars and as the trial went on the details of what had actually happened that fateful morning began to unravel. In the meantime, the trial of her twin sister, Jasmiyah, was set for a later date that same year. During the proceedings, details of what happened were provided by Rockdale D. A., Richard R. Read who repeated what Tas had apparently told prosecutors.

On the day of the killing, Tas and Jas had awoken and come downstairs ready for school. Their mother was already downstairs in the kitchen. Apparently, Jarmecca had a pot in her hand and she hit Jas with it. At that point Tas grabbed the pot but Jarmecca then reached for a knife. This was where the fighting began and involved everything from name calling to scratching and biting. During the chaos, according to the reports, Jarmecca was cut with the knife. She then apparently ran out of the house and attempted to get assistance from a neighbour but received no response. Leaving blood at the scene from her cuts, she then decided to go back to her own house – and unfortunately to her death.

Reports claim Jarmecca returned to the house and went back into the kitchen where she sat at the table. However, it wasn't long before she had grabbed the knife again in order to resume the fight with the two girls. As the fight continued Jarmecca sustained a variety of injuries, one of which proved fatal. When she was found, the young mother had been stabbed in the lungs, jugular and the neck. This had led to the spinal cord being severed, which was the fatal injury that ended her young life.

Read went on to state that the girls then continued to school, although they were obviously late. They flagged the police vehicle down later that afternoon and came up with the story of finding their mother's body in the home.

Dysfunctional family

A number of people had described the Whiteheads as being a dysfunctional family. Apparently, Jarmecca and the twins used to live with their great-grandmother Della Frazier but then Jarmecca had decided to move in with a boyfriend and took the twins with her. While the girls were grade A students at one time, their grades apparently began to slide and they became increasingly difficult and unruly. It is alleged that they became fed up of their mother preaching about boys and drugs as the girls found this hypocritical because of the lifestyle she led herself. This led to increasing animosity and resulted in the incident that had led to the girls being sent back to their great-grandmother's home in 2008.

Read also read out a statement from a counsellor who had worked with the girls and their mother in a bid to try and reconcile them. He basically said that the Whitehead family appeared to 'thrive in chaos'. He said that all generations of the family found it difficult to take responsibility for their role in family problems that arose. He also said that the teens had not been given proper guidance from adults in the family.

He went on to state that Jas had actually told counsellors that if she was forced to move back in with her mother, she would end up killing her. Of course, this threat wouldn't have been taken seriously at the time but chillingly it came to fruition all too soon.

During the trial, Lynda Whitehead, Jarmecca's mother and the girls' grandmother, addressed the court. She said that although she had seen that the twins were getting out of control she had never feared them or suspected they would be violent. She added that she had loved her daughter and she loved her granddaughters, so there were 'no winners' in this case. She also went on to say that unfortunately, Jas and Tas had never been taught what was right and what was wrong.

In a poignant comment to Tas during the trial, Judge Irwin stated: "Tragedy of epic proportions. I never knew what that meant until today."

Victim – Jarmecca "Nikki" Whitehead

GRETCHEN GRAHAM AND GLORIA FRANKLIN

Gretchen Graham and Gloria Franklin were identical twins but with very different lifestyles. While one led a relatively normal life, the other twin lived a life filled with chaos. Despite these differences, one thing that both twins had in common was allowing the death of Gretchen's four-year-old son, Shawn.

Little Shawn Graham died tragically in a fire

When we talk about evil twins, most people think of twins that have cold-bloodedly planned and carried out a killing or even multiple killings. However, this is not necessarily the case, as the story of Gretchen Graham and Gloria Franklin demonstrates. This case shows that in some instances it is not the act that the perpetrator carries out to cause harm to someone that is evil but the act that they fail to carry out in order to save them.

Gretchen Graham and Gloria Franklin were twin sisters, and like other identical twins had a lot in common. However, as they grew older their lifestyles changed radically and they took very different routes in life. Both of the twins did struggle with a very difficult childhood and both were intellectually challenged. By the time they were in their twenties, Gloria was leading a relatively normal life, although both twins are said to have been suffering from mental issues to some degree. Gretchen took a very different path in life to her twin sister – a life of chaos and disorganisation, which eventually led to an unplanned pregnancy and the birth of a son in 1985.

After giving birth to her son, who she named Shawn, Gretchen struggled to bring the child up, as her own lifestyle was so chaotic. The life that Shawn was born into was one that no child would want to have to cope with let alone a toddler. However, while other small kids were enjoying being looked after by their parents in a warm home with food, love and comfort on tap, little Shawn was living from hand to mouth and was often homeless and neglected. On many occasions, he was left to his own devices without any adult supervision while his mother did her own thing and simply didn't acknowledge Shawn.

Moving in with her twin

The troubled Gretchen Graham was struggling to cope on her own along with a young son to look after, particularly with the less than ideal lifestyle that she led. Her young son was not looked after properly, often had no home or food, and was generally neglected. It is little wonder that the youngster therefore started acting up now and again, which caused his mother even more problems. Eventually, Gretchen turned to her more sensible twin sister for help. She and Shawn then moved in with her twin sister and her sister's husband in the Wolverine Lake area.

Wolverine Lake Area

Unfortunately, there is not a lot documented about the case and many of the facts surrounding the incident remain unknown. What is known is that little Shawn sometimes played up because of the way in which he had been brought up. The twins' response to this was to punish the boy by locking him in his room at Gloria's home for long periods at a time. There was a padlock on the outside of the door and the young boy was forced to remain inside the room until the sisters decided that he had been punished enough and let him out.

However, it was one such punishment that led to tragedy in 1989, when Shawn was just four years of age. According to reports, Shawn had a habit of picking things up such as lighters and then using them to create small fires. This sort of behaviour stemmed from the neglect and lack of motherly love he had experienced in the first few years of his life. His mother and her twin did not know how to handle his behaviour, so he was generally punished by being locked away.

As was the norm when he had acted up, the sisters had locked him in his room on December 11th 1989. Both Gretchen and Gloria were in the house that evening, as was Gloria's husband. While locked in his room, the four year old must have come across one of the lighters that he'd taken and before long he'd set fire to something which resulted in him starting a blaze that was set to spiral out of control. However, when the adults in the house realized that he had started a fire and was effectively locked in his room burning and choking, not one of them lifted a finger to help. His cries were ignored by his mother, his aunt and his uncle, and the unfortunate child was left to perish.

Twins on trial

In what was a truly harrowing case resulting in the tragic loss of such a young life, the twins were found guilty of second degree murder. While they may not have physically killed the young boy with their own hands, they had let him die by failing to try and free him from the room in which he was locked when the fire started. Not only this, but they made no attempt to call for help.

On December 21st, both twins pleaded guilty as charged and were sentenced by Oakland County Circuit Judge Edward Sosnick. The twins were just 28 years of age at the time. According to the attorney acting on behalf of Gretchen Graham, the reason why she hadn't made any attempt to rescue her son or call for help was because she was borderline retarded. The attorney acting on behalf of her twin sister, Gloria Franklin, also stated that his client had mental issues that had impacted on her actions that fateful evening.

Whatever the reasons behind the twins deciding to let poor Shawn perish in a fire in what was effectively his prison, the judge decided that they had to pay the price. They were both sentenced to between eight and forty years behind bars.

JOEL AND MICHAEL STOVALL

Just over two weeks after the devastating 9/11 terrorist attacks in America, another horrific event took place involving the death of a Sheriff's deputy, a shootout, and two killers on the loose – evil twins, Joel and Michael Stovall

The Stovall twins

On September 11th 2001, the world watched in horror as a day of devastating terrorist attacks began with a commercial aircraft ploughing into the side of one of the World Trade Centre twin towers. That day, thousands of lives were lost and not only the country but the world mourned what went on to become one of the most horrific terrorist attacks in history.

Just over two weeks after the attacks, another horrific incident was taking place in Fremont County. However, this was not down to a group of terrorists but two young men aged just 24 – twin brothers, Joel and Michael Stovall. These evil twins kicked off the night of 28th September 2001 with the coldblooded shooting of a dog. By the time they had finished, one deputy was dead, other officers had been injured, and the authorities were caught up in a high speed chase and shootout.

The incident finished with the brothers being captured and sentenced to life imprisonment plus 896 years, meaning that they will certainly spend the rest of their days inside. However, authorities and the community in general were so appalled by the crimes these brothers committed that many were up in arms over the fact that they were not given the death penalty.

A night of terror begins

On September 28th 2001, the residents of the United States – and indeed people from all over the planet – were still reeling from the horrific events of 9/11. The death toll was continuing to mount and the horror just never seemed to end as emergency services continued to try and address the devastation that had rocked the country. However, for people in the Fremont County area, the terror was set to continue all because of the crimes committed by deadly duo Joel and Michael Stovall.

The evening of terror began on September 28th in Penrose, when Joel Stovall took a gun and fired five bullets into his neighbour's dog, killing the animal. The officer that was called to the scene following the shooting was Deputy Jason Schwartz, who arrested Stovall for reckless endangerment. A number of Joel's family members came out at that point in order to defend him, and this included his twin brother Michael Stovall. Michael apparently went as far as to threaten the deputy according to reports, and Schwartz then decided to call for backup, which duly arrived. At this point, Joel had already been put into the back of the patrol car and before long Michael joined him. Little did Schwartz know that in a short space of time he would become the second victim of the evening at the hands of these evil twins.

According to reports, it appears that Michael was not searched properly before being placed into the back of Schwartz's vehicle with his brother. This was a massive oversight, as it later transpired that the twin had two handguns on his person along with a homemade handcuff key. With these items on hand, it was inevitable that tragedy would strike.

Officers attacked

After the two brothers were placed into the patrol vehicle, Schwartz began to drive to the jail where the twins were being transported. However, while he was driving, Michael got busy with the makeshift handcuff key and then took out his guns, which included a 32 calibre semiautomatic and a 9mm semiautomatic. As Schwartz continued to drive, he was taken by complete surprise and shot in the back of the head. This obviously caused him to lose control of the vehicle, which skidded into a ditch. The evil brothers then dragged the dying deputy from the patrol car and shot him another sixteen times before taking off on foot to Florence.

Victim – Jason Scott Schwartz

In Florence, the two brothers were hiring a trailer and this was filled with firearms and weaponry. When they reached the trailer, the twins grabbed a wide variety of weapons, arming themselves to the hilt. They also stole a neighbour's truck. In the meantime the police chief at Florence Police Department had heard about the murder of Schwartz and sent two of his officers out to the trailer to check out the situation.

As the officers approached the trailer, Joel and Michael opened fire. One officer, Toby Bethal, was shot a number of times close to his spine and he ended up crashing his car into a tree.

While he did not die from his injuries he was left paralysed and would spend the coming years trying to make some sort of recovery. Even now, he is confined to a wheelchair and has undergone a number of surgical procedures.

Tony Bethal was left paralysed by the evil twins

The chase continues

After shooting at the officers that came to check out the trailer, the twins used the stolen truck to head towards Canon City. They were being pursued by officers at the time and the Florence Police Chief, Mike Ingle, said that at one point he actually caught up with the truck but one of the twins opened fire and bullets were fired at the patrol car. One hit Ingle in the arm.

When they reached Canon City, the twins continued to exchange gunfire with police officers and authorities continued to chase them onto U.S.50. In addition to continuing with the gunfire, the brothers also started throwing items out of the truck to try and cause injuries and accidents to the officers that were giving chase. One patrol vehicle was disabled after being hit by a typewriter that was thrown from the truck.

The high speed chase continued through the county, with the brothers firing their weapons at officers as they continued to try and escape. However, as they came close to arriving in Salida they came upon a roadblock and were forced to turn back. Just half a mile or so after turning back, they stopped the truck, abandoned it and headed off into the mountains on foot. Police officers waited further back for the brothers to come back – had they tried to approach the abandoned vehicle more of them would have been injured or killed, as it was later revealed that the twins had set up an ambush just above the truck.

What followed then was a 24 hour manhunt for the twins, which included the use of tactical teams and a helicopter. The following evening, on September 29th, Joel and Michael Stovall tried to approach their abandoned truck again. However, there were officers there waiting to pounce and at last the two brothers were apprehended and captured.

The twins are charged

On November 2nd, the two brothers were charged and promptly entered into a plea agreement. They pleaded guilty to first degree murder, aggravated robbery, and numerous counts of attempted first degree murder. Each of them received life without parole plus 896 years. However, despite this sentence there were still many people who were unhappy that they were not handed down the death sentence. One official said that one of the reasons for this was because it was impossible to determine which of the twins did what, which would make it hard to sentence them both to death. This is a problem that authorities often have with identical twins who share the same appearance and the same DNA.

In 2009, Joel Stovall launched an appeal to try and have his sentence reduced, stating that his defence counsel improperly coerced a guilty plea. However, the judge hearing the appeal was

not convinced and Joel's bid for a reduced
sentence failed.

BETTY WILSON AND PEGGY LOWE

When popular Huntsville surgeon, Jack Wilson, was found beaten and stabbed to death, the whole community was shocked. They were even more shocked when it appeared that the person that had arranged his murder was his own wife, Betty, and her twin sister Peggy.

Betty Wilson and Peggy Lowe

In May 1992, the residents of an affluent and tight-knit community in Huntsville were shocked to learn that a hugely popular and pleasant resident had died. It wasn't just the fact that the resident – a prominent surgeon – had died that devastated the community of Boulder Circle but the realisation that he had actually been murdered.

Dr. Jack Wilson was a pleasant, cheerful man who was well-liked and very much respected. He was married to Betty, who he met at the hospital where he worked in 1974. She had been a nurse at the same hospital and once they married they became a well-known couple around the area and hobnobbed with the likes of politicians and journalists.

The marriage seemed to be a very happy one to the outside world, but it appears that the couple may have been putting on something of a brave face. In reality things were starting to slide, which is why on that Memorial Day weekend in 1992 Jack Wilson was making plans to take his wife on a trip away to Santa Fe. Planned for the following day, Wilson was hoping that the romantic break could help to bring them both closer together again.

Betty's promiscuous lifestyle

While Jack Wilson's focus was on trying to get things back on track with his wife, Betty, her mind was most definitely elsewhere. A former alcoholic, she had been persuaded by her husband to attend Alcoholics Anonymous meetings, and while this certainly helped with her drinking it also provided her with easy access to a long line of vulnerable men.

As a result of her meetings at AA, Betty gave up drinking altogether, which must have delighted her husband. What wouldn't have delighted him, however, was the fact that she was using the meeting to meet and invite a variety of recovering alcoholics back to their marital home for fun and games in the bedroom.

Bizarrely, when he did find out about Betty's infidelities, 55-year-old Dr. Wilson tried to turn a blind eye. He would tell his wife 'it's just sex' and let her get on with it. According to reports, he felt guilty and blamed himself because he suffered from Crohn's Disease, which meant that he was impotent. If they did engage in any sexual activity, the use of mechanical objects had to be employed. In addition to this he worked lengthy hours and this left his wife of seventeen years free to drive around in her sporty car looking for other means of entertainment.

Betty had been brought up in Gadsden, Alabama, along with her twin sister. Her sister, Peggy Lowe, was now a respected schoolteacher as well as a practicing and churchgoing Christian. After meeting Jack, who was a doctor at the hospital where she worked in Alabama, Betty found herself in a socially exciting and financial secure situation and living in a nice home in a great neighbourhood. However, seventeen years on, although she still wanted all of those benefits, the one thing she didn't want was the person that was providing it all for her.

It was later to emerge that she had shown clear signs of jealousy to a friend whose husband had passed away and left his entire estate to her. The friend was still quite young and said that Betty seemed envious of her situation.

Discovering the body

Some of the neighbours of Jack and Betty Wilson in Boulder Circle saw the good doctor arrive home from work on the afternoon of May 22nd 1992. Apparently, he seemed in high spirits and he busied himself doing some jobs around the large mansion that they lived in so that he could get ready for their trip away the following day. This was the last time that those neighbours saw Jack Wilson alive.

Later that evening, Betty Wilson arrived back home from one of her AA meetings. She entered the house as usual but a few minutes later she went banging on a neighbour's door clearly distraught. Apparently, after entering the house she had discovered the body of her husband outside the bedroom door. He had been beaten and stabbed to death.

Betty and the neighbour called 911 and police were promptly dispatched to the mansion. In a matter of minutes, officers came across the body of Dr. Wilson. There was a baseball bat lying close to the body and the doctor had also been stabbed. It was presumed that the doctor had walked in on an intruder who was intending to burgle the property. The doctor must have surprised the intruder, who then used a baseball bat to beat him and a knife to deal the final fatal blows.

However, it wasn't long before police realised that there were no actual signs of any break-in, so how did this intruder get into the property in the first place? They quickly came to the conclusion that it was not in fact a burglar that had killed Dr. Wilson but somebody who he already knew – and who had easy access to the house.

Investigating the family

One of the many tasks that the police now had to do was investigate the family to see whether any of them might have had the cause and the ability to commit the crime. Betty Wilson was, of course, amongst those to be checked out. Police looked at credit card receipts as well as talking to eyewitnesses in order to get an idea of where she was all day on the date of Jack's death. Pretty much the whole day was accounted for apart from a couple of very short periods of around half an hour, one at 2.30pm and the other from 5pm.

Police also checked out other family members but drew a blank with each one, as they all appeared to have rock solid alibis for the day of the murder. However, police were about to get the big break that they were waiting for. Officials from the Shelby County Sheriff's Office called investigators to say that the previous week they'd received a call from a woman who had expressed concern for a friend. She said that this rather troubled friend, who was an alcoholic amongst other things, had told her that he had been hired by someone to kill a doctor in Huntsville. The person that is supposed to have recruited him for this grisly task was a woman by the name of Peggy Lowe. The ultimate big break for investigators would come when they realised that Peggy Lowe was actually the twin sister of the doctor's widowed wife, Betty.

White's Story

After discovering that Peggy was Betty's twin sister, police were quick to look up the man who claimed to have been recruited for the murder, James Dennison White. The 42 year old was not only a drunk who was full of tall tales but also suffered from mental disorders as well as being a drug abuser. The woman who had told authorities of what he'd told her had actually admitted that she didn't really believe him because he was always coming out with strange stories. However, she had decided to contact police after hearing about the death of Jack Wilson in the news.

White had already been on the wrong side of the law a number of times for crimes ranging from drug peddling through to kidnap. He was regularly evaluated while behind bars and one of the latest assessments had him down as suffering from delusions and being unable to tell the difference between reality and fantasy.

Nevertheless, police had to question White and to start with he denied everything. However, as time went on he started to fall over himself in terms of what he was telling officers. As his claims and stories started to unravel, White eventually gave up the ghost and admitted that he had been hired by both Peggy Lowe and Betty Wilson to carry out the murder. Over the coming weeks, more and more detail was to be revealed by White, building a shocking picture of how a promiscuous woman and her churchgoing sister had plotted and planned the murder of a respected doctor.

According to White, he was doing some carpentry work at a local elementary school and this is where he met Peggy Lowe, who was a teacher there. They became friendly and she asked him to carry out some work at her house. He claims that eventually, during one of the long chats that they started to have, she told him that she wanted to have her husband killed. She then told him that it was actually her sister that wanted to hire someone to kill her husband. White apparently told her that he knew someone that could do it for $20,000 but Peggy told him that was too much. Eventually, a price of $5,000 was agreed upon and Peggy is said to have given White half of this amount in a bag containing small bills.

Over the following weeks, White continued to provide police with details of what he claimed had happened. This included various phone calls between himself and the two sisters, details of a gun that was given to him by the twins, and the handing over of expense money, some of which was given to him inside a library book.

He went on to tell police that on May 22nd, the day of the murder, Betty Wilson had picked him up from a parking lot between 5pm and 5.30pm and taken him to the house. He hadn't brought the gun with him, as he didn't like them but he did have some rope with him. Betty left him in the house to wait for her husband and to get the job done, and she went back out again. He waited about two hours in the property alone before the doctor showed up.

He went on to tell officers that although he did remember grappling with the doctor for the baseball bat, he did not recall killing him. He also took police to his property, where they found the gun, which was registered to Betty White, and a library book that was checked out in her name.

White

Twins arrested

In 1993, based upon the statements that had
been made by White, police believed that they
had enough information to arrest both Betty and
Peggy over the death of Jack Wilson. This sent
shockwaves through the community, as Betty
was a highflying socialite with plenty of money
and involvement in fundraising. Her twin was a
churchgoing school teacher who led a quiet life.
They seemed an unlikely pair to be plotting
murder. However, there was always the fact that
the doctor's estate, which Betty was set to
inherit, was said to be worth around $6 million...

In the meantime, James White was given a
proposal by the District Attorney. He was told
that if he helped authorities to convict the twins
he would not face the electric chair but would
instead get a custodial sentence with the chance
of parole within just seven years. This deal
created a lot of controversy and publicity around
the world, as did every other aspect of the case.

One of the issues that caused controversy was
that, although White had made a detailed
confession to police about the involvement of the
twins, there was nothing that physically linked
him to the crime scene and he had never been
seen with Betty Wilson. While prosecutors said
that Betty's affairs and the fact that she stood to
inherit the estate was enough to provide a
motive, many did not think that there was enough
evidence available. In the meantime, the
relatives of Jack Wilsons started their own legal

action to try and stop Betty from inheriting any of his estate.

The trial of Betty and Peggy

When the twin's trial began, controversy and publicity reached boiling point. Even movie agents were coming to town in order to try and secure movie rights to the story while the media was having a field day printing all sorts of stories. In the end, the trial was moved to Tuscaloosa as a result of the frenzy of publicity and activity.

Of course, Betty and Peggy had denied fervently that they'd had any involvement with White or the killing or Dr. Wilson but officials really had their work cut out for them in terms of working out who was telling the truth. While the gun and book belonging to Betty Wilson had been found in White's property, it was argued that he could have stolen them from the property. There was also concern over the amount of times that White had changed his story and it was claimed that he could be telling investigators whatever they wanted to hear in order to get a jail sentence rather than a death one. At one point, when there was doubt being cast on whether prosecutors had enough evidence to convict the twins, White summoned officers from his jail cell and told them that he had just remembered that while has was at the mansion following the murder he'd changed his clothes and then put his old clothes in a carrier bag, which was the same bag that Mrs. Lowe had given him money in. He told them exactly where they could find this

carrier with his other clothes in – hidden close to
the swimming pool. Authorities did indeed find
the bag, but there was a lot of suspicion in
relation to why it hadn't been found the first time
around. In addition, forensics was unable to find
any bloodstain evidence on them. Many believed
that White had got someone to plant the bag
there to back up his story and escape the death
sentence.

On the other hand, there were witnesses who
claimed that Betty Wilson had told them that she
wanted her husband dead. There were also
witnesses who confirmed that Betty had been
taking various men to her home for sex while her
husband was alive. These and a range of other
arguments from both the prosecution and the
defense made it extremely difficult for the jury to
work out who to believe. This just added fuel to
the fire in terms of the publicity factor, with the
case now capturing both national and
international attention.

Outcome

Even the outcome of the trial in the case of Betty
Wilson and Peggy Lowe continued to cause a
huge amount of controversy. Betty's trial was on
March 22nd 1993 and the jury deliberated for
nearly two days after hearing all of the evidence
and witness testimonies. Betty Wilson was found
guilty and imprisoned for life without the chance
of parole.

Betty Wilson found guilty

Peggy Lowe's trial was set for six months later. Again, the jury heard all of the evidence and witnesses took to the stand. All of the testimonies and evidence in Peggy's trial was pretty much the same as in her sister's trial. However, in this case it was suggested that two people may have been involved in the killing and that it may not have even taken place in the property or involved the use of the baseball bat. There was also a new jury in this trial.

This time around, the outcome was quite different. The jury took less than three hours to reach a decision and they found Peggy Lowe not guilty. Peggy had come across as a good, helpful, Christian woman in court while her sister had been portrayed as evil according to reports. Even the prosecutor in the case said that he'd felt like he was 'fighting God'.

In the meantime, White has continued to make changes to his story and at one point even tried to retract his statements altogether, stating that he'd never met Lowe or Wilson before. Another time, he changed the time at which Wilson is supposed to have picked him up from the parking lot to take him to the mansion. He'd originally said it was between 5.00 and 5.30pm, when her whereabouts had been unaccounted for by police. However, he then changed this to between 6.00 and 6.30pm, when her whereabouts was already accounted for. Based on these changes of heart, Betty Wilson continues to appeal her conviction and there are various support websites that have sprung up claiming that when they jury found Betty guilty they effectively put an innocent woman behind bars.

Victim – Dr. Jack Wilson

EDWIN AND EDWARD BERNDT

Classed as unstable and insane, twin brothers Edwin and Edward Berndt spent three months living normally in their home...with the decomposing body of their mother lying face down on the floor.

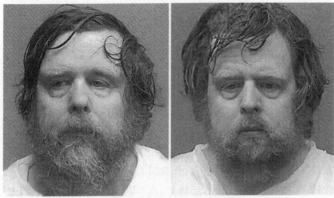

The Berndt twins

On January 10th 2011, identical twin brothers Edwin and Edward Berndt were in the home that they shared with their mother, Sybil Berndt. The two brothers were sat in the living room of the house in southeast Houston watching a BCS Championship college football game. While the two brothers were sitting enjoying the game, their elderly mother, who was 88 years of age, came into the room. She seemed to be somewhat delusional when she walked in and was going on about how someone was trying to break into the property and steal the piano.

As she was ranting about the possibility of someone breaking in, the old woman suddenly fell to the floor – at least, this is what the Berndt twins told authorities later down the line after an investigation into the incident that was about to occur was launched. According to the twins, after their mother fell to the floor she did not get back up again. While the twins must have known that something was wrong, they decided that they weren't going to take any action because they did not have enough money to get medical attention and care for their mother.

As a result of the twins' decision, Sybil Berndt was left lying on the floor in the Houston property for three days. For some reason, not only did the twins not seek medical assistance for their mother but they also did not provide her with any food or water while she was incapacitated on the floor. On January 12th 2011 it was Sybil Berndt's 89th birthday. However, she spent her birthday continuing to lie incapacitated on the floor without food or water as her two sons got on with their day to day lives. The following day, January 13th 2011, Sybil Berndt died.

Living with the body

Following the death of their elderly mother on the floor of their home, the Berndt twins made a bizarre decision. They had decided not to get any help or assistance for their mother while she lay dying for three days because they couldn't afford it according to statements that they later made to police. Now that she was actually dead, they decided that that they couldn't afford a burial or funeral so they left the body where it was.

For the next three months, the twins simply got on with their day to day lives leaving their mother's body to rot in the property. Police later stated that they must have been stepping over the body at least several times a day in order to get around. Neither of the twins had worked for some years, so they also would have spent long periods of time in the property with their mother's body right beneath their noses.

For several months, the brothers continued to live in the house with the rotting body of their dead mother. However, in April 2011 the police were alerted because neighbours were starting to get concerned about the fact that Sybil had not been seen or heard of in a few months. An officer was despatched to the Houston property to run a welfare check on the old lady, but she was not prepared for what she would find.

The body is finally found

Following a call from a concerned neighbour in April 2011, a police officer called at the Berndt house to check whether Sybil Berndt was okay. What she found made it clear that the old lady was most certainly not okay. After knocking at the door, the officer was finally admitted to the house by the Berndt twins – initially they had refused to let anyone in. What the officer found was the rotting corpse of their dead mother lying face down in the foyer with the dressing gown pulled up under her arms and no underwear on.

Moreover, Edward and Edwin had turned off the air conditioning in the property, which had caused even faster decomposition of the corpse. There was a distinct stench of rotting flesh throughout the property that the brothers had continued living in for three months following the demise of their mother. Even officers said that the stench was difficult to stomach for more than a minute or two without heaving, yet the brothers had managed to live, sleep and eat in these conditions for months.

After the body was found, a search of the property was also carried out. From documents and papers that were found, it was discovered that Sybil had a lot of money stashed away in accounts – around $700,000 in total according to reports. She was, by all accounts, a wealthy widow whose husband had passed away from Alzheimer's a few years earlier and whose income came mainly from a ranch property that the family owned and rented out.

Twins questioned

Neighbours were, of course, shocked to learn of the death of Sybil Berndt. Many had become concerned between January and April because of the lack of activity at the ranch style property and because there had been no sign of the old lady. Many had described her as being very kind hearted and always looking out for others. Neighbours also described the twins as being very docile and keeping themselves to themselves.

The twins were both wearing flannel pyjamas when the police showed up that April day, and they told officers that they had not even left the property for a few months. Apparently, they had been living on whatever food they could find in the home, which appeared to consist of candy, popcorn and potato chips.

The twins also told investigators that for around one day after she fell to the floor their mother was actually able to talk although she was clearly unable to get up. An officer later asked the twins why they didn't seek help for their injured or ill mother. They replied it was because she never asked them to.

While both men were looking somewhat blank when they were interviewed, officials did say that they both seemed pretty intelligent. Both of them had completed High School and Edward was even in a special program for gifted children while at school. However, some family members stated that the brothers were actually mentally disabled.

Out on bond for evaluation

Following the discovery of Sybil Berndt's body in April 2011, her two sons, twins Edward and

Edwin, were taken in and interviewed. They were then charged with felony murder after it was revealed that they left their mother dying on the floor of the property for three days and failed to seek help. They then left her rotting body in the property for several months until it was discovered by police.

After they were arrested and charged, the bonds for the brothers were set at $500,000 each by the judge. However, this was soon reduced to $30,000 each and pretty soon the brothers were out on bond. They were then taken to a secure place in order to be evaluated. Officials said that it was important for the men to be checked so that they could get a better idea of the extent of any mental disability.

In the meantime, another court hearing was set for later that year and in the meantime assessments of the brothers were carried out by professionals. In July of that year, a Grand Jury came together and the Berndt brothers were 'no billed' which meant that they would not face charges for the death of their mother. Instead, a guardian was assigned for the twins and they were moved into assisted accommodation in a bid to get them the help that professionals deemed they needed following their evaluations.

Some stated that had the twins let their mother die out of malicious intent, they would have behaved differently to the way they did. For example, they would have dragged the body into another room or even put it in the refrigerator. As

one pointed out, they had no proper food in the
house so there would have been plenty of room
in the fridge.

Conclusion

As these ten cases show, evil twins have committed a variety of crimes over the years ranging from rape and assault through to manslaughter and murder. In some cases, such as the deaths of Shawn Graham and Sybil Berndt, the twins in question did not commit a crime through their physical actions but through their failure to take action, which resulted in tragic death.

While these types of crimes are committed by individuals pretty much every day somewhere in the world, we seem to find it all the more fascinating when there are twins involved. Most of us probably wonder whether it is something that is in the blood, particularly when we read about cases such as the Spahalski twins, where one murdering twin didn't even know that the other had also been engaging in murder.

Of course, there are also many other cases where there is only one twin that commits evil crimes while the other becomes a constructive and valued member of society, such as the Calzacorto twins. However, one problem that authorities tend to have with cases such as these is working out which is the evil twin and which is the good one. With identical twins sharing the same appearance and the same DNA, things can get extremely tricky for investigators, authorities and even witnesses.

Thankfully, most sets of twins in this world share nothing more than their appearances, their DNA, and a very close bond. However, like the ones documented in this book there are a minority that also share something far more sinister – an urge to commit crimes and even to murder.

Coming Soon

Jon Lawson is currently working on his Serial Killer Series. If you wish you get updates when these are released and are on flash sales please let us know your interest by sending us a message and your email address at www.queenbeespublishing.com

Russian Serial Killers
Australian Serial Killers
Britain Serial Killers
Worst Cannibal Serial Killers in History

IMAGE SOURCES

Case 1: Maskell Twins:
http://img.thesun.co.uk/aidemitlum/archive/00183/SNN0333A_183687a.jpg
Map -
http://www.itraveluk.co.uk/maps/england/690/greater-london/edmonton.html
Dwane Johnston – http://www.murderpedia.org

Case2: Spahalski Twins: www.crimelibrary.com
http://www.dailymotion.com/video/xi4zrq_spahalski-twin-arrested-in-elmira_news
Map - http://www.bestplaces.net/city/new-york/elmira

Case 3: Bondurant Twins: https://s-media-cache-ak0.pinimg.com/236x/04/45/84/0445845d88e425cbc132c6d31742f96f.jpg
https://mylifeofcrime.files.wordpress.com/2014/03/pete-bondurant.jpg
Gwen Dugger -
https://mylifeofcrime.wordpress.com/2014/03/27/deadly-duo-kenneth-patterson-pat-bondurant-and-hugh-pete-bondurant-jr-terrorized-giles-county-tn-in-1986/
House -
http://photos.al.com/4558/gallery/pete_and_pat_bondurant_feature/index.html#/3

Case 4: Spitzer Twins: http://4.bp.blogspot.com/-zO_oEVMtY/U1OmWcbpcHI/AAAAAAAAAIc/S06z47vWGT0/s1600/1383875_68795183788940 0_1511796385_n.jpg

World café - http://www.yelp.ie/biz_photos/world-
cafe-santa-monica-
3#rYHaPLbaZhSV3w3uJ7oolA
Rohypnol -
http://noupoort.co.za/content/rohypnol

Case 5: Sotolongo Twins:
http://archive.news10.net/images/300/169/2/asse
tpool/images/130225094424_Sotolongo-Tyrone-
Jerone-1280.jpg
Victory Park - http://stockton-
central.news10.net/news/crime/104808-stockton-
residents-mourn-murder-victim-victory-park

Case 6: The Whitehead Twins:
http://www.gannett-cdn.com/-mm-
/b59b9877b6cfe4d3140abd6f01a473bb02aafded
/c=0-2-848-639&r=x404&c=534x401/local/-
/media/WXIA/WXIA/2014/08/01/1406911331000-
1400187033000-twinss.jpg
Nikki Whitehead -
http://www.rockdalenews.com/archives/2245/

Case 7: Gretchen Graham and Gloria Franklin:
http://upload.wikimedia.org/wikipedia/commons/e
/ea/Fire_in_the_dark.JPG
Wolverine Park Area -
https://www.google.ie/maps/place/Wolverine+Lak
e,+Commerce+charter+Township,+MI,+USA/dat
a=!4m2!3m1!1s0x8824a5b60ac1a9d3:0x6dce66f
41cff01ba?sa=X&ei=yEIIVbTFKZHoaMvkgeAM&
ved=0CIMBEPIBMAw

Case 8: Joel and Michael Stovall:
https://mylifeofcrime.files.wordpress.com/2013/0
3/michaelstovall-prison-mug.jpg
Jason Scott Schwartz and crashed car –
www.dailyrecord.com
Tony Bethal - https://a2-
images.myspacecdn.com/images03/34/c1b3164
6151e4f54994389284480c52d/300x300.jpg

Case 9: Betty Wilson and Peggy Lowe:
http://www.bing.com/images/search?q=peggy+lo
we+twin&id=04B8FFBCB1A686E6F5E48303B1
BC2ACC00F2DEA4&FORM=IQFRBA#view=det
ail&id=2E6020CF6B6D3CC00997FB90FB00B56
B8C76CCE3&selectedIndex=3
White - http://www.hankford.com/bettywilson/
Dr. Jack Wilson -
http://www.hankford.com/bettywilson/

Case 10: Edwin and Edward Berndt:
http://a.abcnews.com/images/US/ht_Berndt_twin
s_mugshots_dr_110412_wmain.jpg

Printed in Great Britain
by Amazon